I0435361

Being Grateful
Becoming Whole

David Tuffley

To my beloved Nation of Four
Concordia Domi – Foris Pax

"Gratitude bestows reverence, allowing us to encounter everyday epiphanies, those transcendent moments of awe that change forever how we experience life and the world."
— John Milton (English Poet, 1608—74)

Altiora

Published 2015 by Altiora Publications
AltioraPublications.com/

ISBN-13: 978-1507741283 ISBN-10: 1507741286

Copyright © David Tuffley, 2015.
All rights reserved. Without limiting the rights under copyright reserved above, no part of this publication may be reproduced, stored in, or introduced into a retrieval system, or transmitted, in any form without the prior written permission of the copyright owner.

About the Author
David Tuffley PhD is a Lecturer in Applied Ethics & Socio-Technical Studies at Griffith University in Australia. David has written widely on Applied Psychology topics.

Facebook: www.facebook.com/tuffley/

Acknowledgements

I acknowledge the *Turrbal* and *Jagera* indigenous peoples, on whose ancestral land I write this book.

Contents

Introduction

Gratitude – how do we define it? Gratitude is when you feel a strong sense of appreciation for both the tangible and intangible aspects of your life and the world you live in. Coming from the Latin word *gratia*, for grace, gratitude is an elevated state of mind that is rightly called a state of grace. This book describes how you can dwell in this state of grace, and enjoy the many benefits that stem from it.

When you live with an attitude of gratitude, you bring your inner world into harmony with your outer world, recognizing that so much of what nourishes and sustains you in life comes from a source beyond yourself. Gratitude makes you whole in the sense of making you feel part of something much bigger than yourself.

The way that you view the world in which you find yourself is *always* under your control, regardless of how much it might seem others are in control. An optimist sees it one way, a pessimist a quite different way; same situation, two different perceptions.

An attitude of gratitude is an essentially optimistic one in which you are in the daily habit of noticing that there is *always* something good, something of benefit to be found in any situation. It may not be what you want, but you understand that it is what you *need* in order to grow into a fuller expression of yourself. The world is providing for your needs, not pandering to your wants.

This providential view of the world, and the appreciation that goes along with it, allows you to mentally connect with something larger than yourself. This could be with the community that you live in, Nature or a Higher Power. By connecting with this external power, you are transcending your egoic self. Going beyond the ego and connecting with a larger reality outside of yourself is the source of your happiness.

Gratitude has long been recognised by religions and philosophy as a desirable practice, but for many, the connection between gratitude and a sense of well-being is not an obvious one. This book seeks to remedy that, showing you how being grateful can lead you to a deeper sense of satisfaction with your life; something which escapes many people in this age of entitlement, where a culture of complaint creates the opposite of gratitude.

This is not to suggest that you should accept second or third-class service without a murmur. You can still point out where deficiencies exist and have them remedied without losing your positive attitude.

The recognition of the power of gratitude by modern Psychology has been a long time coming. Historically, conventional psychology focuses on what is *wrong* with a person rather than what is *right*. Today, a growing body of research indicates that people with higher levels of gratitude also experience higher levels of subjective well-being and resilience. In other words, you can be happier and less depressed, even when your circumstances are quite modest because you have learned to notice and appreciate the good that is present in every situation. With the incidence of depression in the developed world at an all-time high, this is good news for anyone who struggles with the black dog of depression.

The practice of gratitude also helps you in a general way to deal more resiliently with the set-backs that life serves up. It can give you a sense of control over how you feel about those events. You cannot always control events or what other people do, but you *can* control how you react them, choosing to think in positive, life-affirming ways that can lead you to feel strong and purposeful.

An attitude of gratitude can even help you sleep more soundly, largely because the thoughts that run through your mind just before going to sleep are more likely to be positive helping you into a peaceful sleep.

Gratitude is an idea that has come full circle. The Roman philosopher Cicero believed that *gratitude is not only the greatest of the virtues but the parent of all others*. More recently the positive psychology movement in has come to embrace this idea in the 21st Century.

Chapter 1:
Research on Gratitude

Ongoing research into the psychology of gratitude reveals a strong correlation between gratitude and a sense of well-being and happiness.

Emmons & McCullough

In one study, Emmons and McCullough asked people to keep a journal in which they recorded their thoughts on three distinct topics. One group wrote about the things they were grateful for, the second group about the things that annoyed them, and the third about things that were neither good nor bad.

Ten weeks later, it was clearly evident that the group that wrote about the things they were grateful for were more optimistic and felt better about their lives generally than those who focussed on what annoyed them. These findings strongly indicate the benefits of keeping a gratitude journal.

Martin Seligman

In another study, Martin Seligman tested a sample of more than 400 people with what he called *the gratitude visit*. The participants were asked to think of someone (living) who did something that made a big difference in their life, but which they never properly thanked them for. They wrote a 300 word testimonial to that person. Then they arranged to go visit them in person but not to say why. When they were face-to-face, they read the testimonial to them. Participants reported feelings of intense joy, the effects of which lasted for around a month.

Happier Relationships

In relationships, it has been found that couples who express gratitude to their partner enjoy a happier relationship overall. They will also be more comfortable expressing concerns about the relationship should these arise.

Gratitude deposits emotional capital in a relationship. It makes each partner mindful of having banked a certain amount of good-will that can be drawn-on during times of doubt or difficulty.

In the Workplace

Managers who express appreciation to their staff will generally motivate them to work harder by doing so. Researchers at the Wharton School conducted a study where fund-raisers for the alumni association were divided into two groups. The first did what they always do – phone alumnus and ask for donations. The second group also did this, but in addition were given a talk at the beginning of the day from the director, who told them how grateful she was for their efforts. The two groups worked on alternating days. After one week, the second group had made 50% more calls than the first.

Resilience

While there is more work to be done in the area, the research to date points strongly to there being a strong correlation between gratitude and happiness, particularly when a person is able to accept that life will occasionally serve up difficult or painful situations along with the good things. This mature attitude leads a person to feel a deep sense of gratitude for being alive in the world with the skills they possess and the opportunity to use those skills to best effect.

Chapter 2:
The Mind-Set of Gratitude

People feel and express gratitude in multiple ways. They can apply it to the past (retrieving positive memories and being thankful for elements of childhood or past blessings), the present (not taking good fortune for granted when it comes), and the future (maintaining a hopeful and optimistic attitude). Regardless of the inherent or current level of someone's gratitude, it's a quality that individuals can successfully cultivate further.

Optimism – Learned or Inherent

Optimism is a vital ingredient in the cultivation of gratitude. Having a tendency towards an optimistic or pessimistic outlook in life is something we are born with, but there is plenty of scope to learn to be more optimistic if you happen to fall into the latter category.

Pessimism or the tendency to interpret events in a negative way might be useful in some environments where extreme caution is advisable, but in the majority of situations, that degree of caution is not warranted. Pessimism is not conducive to happiness and well-being. Like *Eeyore* in *Winnie the Pooh*, pessimists are unhappy. They expect the worst to happen and their expectations are usually met.

As Shakespeare wisely observed *"There is nothing either good or bad but thinking makes it so"*-- Hamlet. Whatever happens, it is our mind-set, our outlook that interprets it as either good or bad.

Optimists are in the habit of reacting to events constructively, confidently, seeing them as opportunities for personal growth. An event may have happened once, but it need not happen again because the optimist believes they have the power to change the circumstances that created the event. A pessimist engages in self-blame and probably thinks that they have little or no power to prevent the same thing happening again. Not surprisingly, pessimism has been linked to depression and suicide.

Optimism has been shown to be a factor in how quickly a person heals after a wound or illness. They tend to recover more quickly than pessimists. Optimism has also been shown to improve the function of a person's immune system, making them less likely to get sick in the first place. Pessimism has likewise been shown to depress the immune system, leaving a person more likely to get sick.

If it is possible to sum up the essence of optimism, it is about knowing that you are in control of yourself, your world, and what happens in it. You take the good with the bad, bounce back with resilience when times are hard, and you expect good things to happen.

Your Associates

To become more grateful, it is helpful to seek out and associate with grateful people.

It is simple fact of human nature that we become like the people we associate with. The more time we spend in someone's company, the more like them we become and *vice versa*. This tendency is hard-wired into the human species, largely because in our evolutionary past, survival depended on having a support group around us. The world was a dangerous place, and loners were vulnerable to predation.

The default setting for most people when they get together is to find something to complain about; the boss, the weather, the economy, anything will do. It allows them to have a sense of solidarity with each other; united in misery. Imagine if you were to ask the group to name one thing that they were truly grateful for. You would likely get a lot of blank stares and people making snide comments to each other about you having gone soft in the head. Ask yourself do you really need friends like this? Misery loves company.

Chapter 3:
Cultivating Gratitude

The cultivation of gratitude has long-term and short-term components. The previous chapters described the overall mind-set factors that create the right conditions for gratitude to grow. This chapter outlines some specific techniques that can be put to good use.

Naikan (Inside Looking)

Naikan is a Japanese contemplative practice that is helpful with cultivating gratitude. It literally means *seeing oneself with the mind's eye*, though many would be more familiar with the term introspection.

Naikan works by meditating on three fundamental questions that lead one to an understanding of themselves, their relationships with others and the nature of human existence; *What have I received from __?, What have I given to __?*, and *What troubles and/or difficulties have I caused?"*

Naikan is a reckoning of the give and take, the good and not so good things inherent in every situation. It helps you to see those situations from other perspectives. We naturally think of how a situation affects us, but how often do we ask ourselves honestly how our actions might be impacting on others.

10

As the great Russian writer Leo Tolstoy observed, *"Man need only divert his attention from searching for the solution to external questions and pose the one, true inner question of how he should lead his life, and all the external questions will be resolved in the best possible way."*

The fruits of Naikan, the realisations you have come to, can then be recorded in your gratitude journal.

Gratitude Journal

The act of writing something down has a way of reinforcing ideas in a way that simply thinking about them does not. When you write, you engage more of your mind, different parts of your brain. Keeping a gratitude journal brings ideas into the forefront of your mind.

Keeping a journal is best done as a matter of habit at a particular time of day. A journal captures your fleeting ideas, lets you make plans, establish goals and of course list those gifts and benefits that life has put your way that might otherwise pass unnoticed.

Suitable content for your gratitude journal might include some personal attribute that you have that you are grateful for, or people in your life for which you are thankful. These are people without whom life would be a whole lot harder. The point is, these people are present in everyone's life, and there is always *something* that we can find to be grateful for, even when times are tough. As odd as it might sound, even being able to

11

draw breath is something to be grateful for. We simply need to train ourselves to notice them, and the gratitude journal accomplishes this.

Quality Relationships

A few good quality relationships are arguably better than having hundreds of acquaintances and fair-weather friends. Quality always matters, but the situation is not black and white. There are grades of friend. They can be placed in a series of concentric circles. At the centre is you. In the circle immediately surrounding you are your closest friends. These will be the people who will be supportive no matter what (a friend in need, is a friend indeed), the ones who will stand by you in times of adversity. You may be able to count them on the fingers of one hand, but one is all you really need.

Within this first circle are the people you trust enough to reveal your inner self. When we talk of the gratitude that comes from quality relationships, it is primarily from this circle that it comes, though the second and third circles have something to contribute.

In the second circle are people you think of as friends, but not intimately so. You get together every so often and enjoy their company. In the third circle are people who you know reasonably well and with whom you are on good terms with. You see them less often, but the experience is nonetheless enjoyable. In the fourth circle are acquaintances that you might be on nodding terms with should you pass each other on the footpath. You can have a polite, but superficial conversation with them at a social event.

In the fifth circle are strangers. You don't know them, but you have no hard feelings towards them or bear them any malice.

In the sixth circle are your enemies (if you have any). These are people with whom there is a mutual dislike, hatred even, people who would do you harm if they could get away with it.

The people in your first circle, your real friends, the ones that you can count on the fingers of one or two hands; these are the folks to be truly grateful for. Tell them, or find a way to show them how grateful you are for having them in your life. It will deepen your relationship greatly.

Sense of Purpose

It would be difficult to overstate the importance of having a clear, strong sense of purpose in life; something that gets you out of bed in the morning and pervades your every moment. This purpose strengthens your will to live and finds expression in numerous life-enhancing ways, all of which creates fertile conditions for gratitude to manifest in your thinking.

You may already have a strong sense of purpose, a mission in life, but in case you do not, it can be cultivated by looking for a way to serve the greater good. It may seem strange that having a mission in life involves transcending self-interest and doing what is in the greater good, but the truth of this has been well established over time.

Obviously if you are in a life-threatening situation, then self-preservation will be paramount. Even then, you may be more concerned about saving others, such as one's children. In day-to-day life though, transcending the self is about doing something that contributes to the common good.

As the philosopher Daniel Dennett observed, true happiness is *finding something more important than yourself and devoting your life to it.*

In the evolutionary environment, our purpose in life was simple; to survive long enough to reproduce. In today's complex, highly differentiated world, a bewildering array of possibilities exist which makes it more difficult for a person to know what their special niche is.

Listen to your heart, to the still small voice that whispers in the quietest moments. This is what tells you what your real purpose in life is. Do not be afraid to listen.

Maintain Perspective

There is an old saying that to *know what something is, it is good to know what it is not*. A good perspective for the cultivation of gratitude is one which creates contrast by recalling that there have been times when life was more difficult than it is now. While it is true that life will become more difficult in the future, for now it is tolerable, perhaps even good.

It is helpful to remember that our fortunes swing like a pendulum back and forth from good to not so good. This is the natural order of things. You have some degree of control over the magnitude of the swing, but you cannot eliminate the swing altogether. The only exception here would be to become a hermit, a recluse who stays in their room every day and does absolutely nothing. Every action you take creates a reaction, and this is the engine that drives the pendulum.

So keeping this perspective creates a contrast in your mind between the past and the present and so creates a mind-set conducive to gratitude.

Prayer

For many readers, the concept of prayer is a religious one, some kind of one-way communication between self and an external Deity. A more useful and all-embracing definition for prayer is that it is a dialogue between the egoic self and one's higher self or Deity (if you happen to believe in one).

It is not necessary to believe in an external Deity to engage in prayer. It can be as simple as recognising that some kind of higher power resides within oneself and with which is beneficial to enter into a dialogue. Note that it is a dialogue not a monologue as seen in the more traditional idea of prayer.

To fully appreciate this process, it is necessary to recognise that in an evolutionary sense humans have multi-level brains and therefore multiple levels to our nature. Parts of our brain are analogous to the reptilian brain. We have evolved from these more primitive life-forms and that nature still resides within us and which still exerts its influence at times of savagery.

Then there is the mammalian brain that cares altruistically for our children and loved-ones. That level evolved about 100 million years ago. Then there is the more recently evolved parts of brain, the part that allows us to live in civilised society and perhaps contribute to the greater good. This is the part of our brain that allows us to navigate the fourth dimension of time and engage in meta-cognition (thinking about thinking). No other creature can do this because their brains do not have the structures to allow it.

Many traditions recognise the *microcosm-macrocosm* phenomena; each individual is a smaller representation of the larger world outside. Our internal nature is a reflection of larger Nature outside, and indeed the

Universe. For some, it will be a stretch to accept that they have a miniature version of the entire universe inside them. For others it will feel right and make perfect sense. It is this part of our nature that can be properly recognised as our higher self and prayer is the way we can communicate with it.

So, a prayer of gratitude is not necessarily an expression of religious intent. It is an acknowledgement of the ultimate source of all that you are, and all that you will ever be. It creates a sense of felt connectedness with the macrocosm, building a bridge with your microcosm.

As the great Persian poet Rumi observed, *if you only say one prayer a day, make it 'Thank-You'.*

Mindfulness

Mindfulness or keeping your attention focussed in the present moment is a key aspect of becoming grateful. It allows you to become aware of what the moment contains, and not to gloss over it on the way to the next moment. Once established, the practice of mindfulness opens up the often extraordinary richness of even the most apparently ordinary moment.

You can understand mindfulness as having a vivid, ongoing moment-by-moment awareness of both your inner and outer worlds. You are aware of everything going on around you, becoming alive to the richness of detail that exists in every situation. This helps you to appreciate the good in every situation. And if there is negativity in a situation, you can use it to create a contrast that brings the good aspects into sharper focus.

Mindfulness is being aware but not judgmental; you avoid placing any kind of value judgment on what you are experiencing. This can be difficult after a lifetime of categorising things as good, bad or indifferent. By being judgment-free, you allow your intuition to interpret what it perceives.

Being judgmental takes you down another road, one which often leads to anger and self-righteousness.

Mindfulness could be properly described as *meta-consciousness*; being conscious of your own consciousness. It is made possible by the recently evolved grey-matter in the brain. With it, you are capable of a kind of thinking that no other creature, not even other highly evolved mammals are capable of. For example, you have an awareness of the fourth dimension; time. You not only perceive past, present and future but can make elaborate plans that involve complex sequences of events. Being aware of you own flow of consciousness is another capability that our evolved brains have, but it must be cultivated if it is to work efficiently.

Cultivate 'Flow'

The psychologist Mihály Csíkszentmihályi is well-known for his work on the state of mind known as

Flow. The Flow state is produced by being mindful, as discussed in the previous section. It is a state of mind in which every moment becomes the best moment, where your attention is fully focussed on the now moment and the task at hand. You are completely immersed in what you are doing and enjoying yourself. The experience of Flow is so enjoyable, that it is easy to feel gratitude for it.

Csíkszentmihályi summarised the ingredients of the Flow state in the following way:

- Intense concentration on the present moment.
- Merging of action and awareness.
- Loss of reflective self-consciousness.
- Feeling fully in control of the situation or activity.
- Time speeds up or slows down.
- The activity is rewarding in itself.

How to cultivate Flow. Arrange your work environment so you feel comfortable and safe. Choose a task that is challenging but which you believe is achievable; difficult but not too difficult. As you go about the task, you must be getting moment-by-moment feedback.

If the task is too easy or too difficult, if the environment is dangerous or the consequences of failure are too awful, then the Flow state will not come.

You know you are in the Flow state when you start to really enjoy yourself and your perception of time becomes distorted. Time will seem to speed up or slow down.

Cross-cultural studies show that the qualitative experience of Flow is the same for people around the world, regardless of culture. This suggests that Flow is an innate capability of humans provided the right circumstances exist. The various ways that people get themselves into the Flow state will differ from culture to culture, but the intensely personal and rewarding inner experience remains fundamentally the same.

Csíkszentmihályi thought that certain personality traits predisposed a person to experiencing Flow; curiosity, persistence, low self-centeredness, and a disposition towards doing things for intrinsic reasons only. These predisposing personality factors also apply to the experience of gratitude.

Strategic Non-Action – *Wu Wei*

A mind-set that is aligned with the natural flow of life and which knows when it is better to take no action, is another way that gratitude can be cultivated. It allows you to gratefully observe the passing parade of life in all its varied richness, having relieved yourself of the presumed duty to always be in control.

In Eastern philosophy this is known as *Wu Wei* which literally means *without effort*. In the West we might think of it as strategic non-action. One goes with the flow, does not resist the larger forces that govern a world of which you are a small part and which you are powerless to oppose in any case. You accept the world as it is without judgment and allow it to simply be.

Non-action acknowledges that worldly events are governed by the laws of Nature, and it is often best to simply allow those laws to play out in their own time, in their own way. Taking action can amount to interference with natural processes, which creates its own problems or at least disturbs the natural flow.

In Eastern philosophy, *Wu Wei* is considered a great virtue. When you align yourself with the natural flow of events (the Tao), events unfold easily, without resistance. Your experience of them is deeper and more intuitive because your perception of those events is not being influenced by your reaction to them, or by the reactions of the world to your reactions. By doing this this, we make it all about us.

In cultures where action is favoured over inaction, as is the case in Western cultures, direct action is considered a virtue while inaction little more than laziness or cowardice. This is too black and white; let us be more subtle and nuanced in our understanding -- there is a time for both action and inaction, each in their proper place

Wu Wei describes the natural action that occurs without contrivance or effort. It simply happens. Think of how plants and animals grow, rivers flow and planets orbit. No-one makes them do what they do, it just happens without effort or control, in accordance with the laws of Nature. Emulating this effortless action requires much patience but can produce a strong feeling of happiness and gratitude because you feel yourself connected with something much larger than yourself.

Not Taking Offence

Though it is phrased in the negative, *not taking offence* is a gratitude-producing mental habit that creates a clear, easy space in which to live your life. Learning the basics is not difficult, but to perfect it might take a lifetime.

The essence of this practice is to not mind what happens and to consciously avoid reacting; easier said than done, when it can seem like it is allowing a bully to push you around. It is to understand that there are non-confrontational ways of dealing with the bully that are ultimately more effective and which do not reduce you to their level. It is a practical application of the strategic non-action principle discussed in the previous section.

Seen from another angle, not taking offence is about having *low expectations*. In a world where people live with a sense of entitlement that was unimaginable only a few decades ago, this can be a challenge. We have base-lined our expectations at such a high level that we are setting ourselves up to be upset by what happens in the world.

Contributing to this sense of entitlement is the way the commercial world places great emphasis on customer satisfaction. Quite right, we think. Surely we have a right to good service. We are paying, after all. But consider how this might be distorting our perception of reality. The people serving us are simply doing a job. They know that if they are to keep their job and continue to be paid; they need to be nice to you. The fact is, many people in service jobs struggle to remain positive in the face of rude, selfish behaviour from customers.

Even if most of the time our high expectations are met through not venturing out of our comfort zone, there will always be times when those expectations will not be met; then you will be aggrieved. Trouble inevitably follows. How *dare* you treat me this way? On the other hand, when your expectations are low, you are seldom disappointed.

There is an enormous pay-off in life satisfaction and gratitude for people who manage to keep their expectations low and accept the world as it is, not as we would like it to be or as we think it ought to be. Not only do they avoid feeling angry, you will see the world in a more realistic light. When you allow the world to be what it is without trying to change it, that acceptance gives you access to an enormous wealth of intuitive knowledge that you can be a great source of enjoyment as you live a happy, harmonious life.

It is not personal

The way people act towards you can seem all-too personal. After all, there they are there in front of you. Their words seem to be directed straight at you. Who could blame you for taking offence at a nasty remark?

In reality, while the other person might be looking straight at you, what they are saying and doing actually has very little to do with you personally. It has everything to do with their own experiences up to that point. They are speaking and acting from the attitudes and assumptions they have built up over many years. You simply managed to trigger a reaction, and now you are in the firing line.

How people react usually follows the pattern that has been established by similar situations in the past. When it is similar to an earlier experience, often from their childhood, then the way that the earlier experience played out will be the template for how *this* situation will go. Mindfulness is the antidote for this problem, giving you the means to rea t appropriately for the situation avoid mindlessly re-enacting the past.

Not taking it personally allows you to not mind what happens and not to be offended. Believe me; ridding yourself of all that negativity is *very* liberating. It frees you up to experience whole new dimensions of life that were previously hidden from you, overlaid by resentment.

There is Beauty All Around

Sometimes you can see it right in front of you, and sometimes you have to look harder for it, but one thing is true, there is beauty all around us. Even in the grimiest prison-yard, a flower can bloom. You just have to train yourself to notice the beauty in all its varied forms; sights, sounds and smells.

Beauty nourishes the soul. Opening yourself to beauty can bring a profound sense of gratitude. For example, on the afternoon that I wrote this, a thunderstorm came across the sky after several months of unseasonably dry weather. The storm was brief, lasting only 10 minutes, but the rain was heavy, and there was much thunder and lightning. When it was over, I went out into the garden. Ah the smell that rises from the earth when it's thirst is slaked, when the rain soaks in. I call it the *grateful earth* smell.

The earth does seem to be grateful at that moment. Down inside, all the processes of life that had lain dormant for months were waking up. They had waited with infinite patience for this rain. The plants and the million tiny creatures living in the earth beneath my feet were grateful, or so I imagined. They would have waited 100 years for the rain's return if necessary.

It might have been easy to take a different perspective, perhaps that soon I would have to dust off the lawn-mower and hedge-trimmer and spend a sweaty hour tending to that same garden when I could have been relaxing in front of the TV. That slightly resentful attitude would be a not uncommon perspective.

That might be an unpleasant prospect for some, but in my own case, in the interests of cultivating a gratitude mind-set, I have changed my thinking to see that there can be enjoyment in performing those chores. After all, being alive and possessed of a healthy body and fully functioning senses is something to be thankful for. It is a matter of perspective.

Aide Memoire

It can be helpful to place reminders in your environment where you will see them often and which remind you to be grateful. Forgetfulness can make us overlook the many reasons we have to be grateful.

Do not fall into the habit of thinking *what have I got to be grateful for? My life is terrible! My partner just left me, I just found out I have a $15,000 tax bill and the doctor tells me I have diabetes...*

There is no disputing that life deals out problems for you to solve. Simply take the view that whatever life is serving up is what you need to be experiencing for your own growth now. When you solve the problem, you will be wiser and stronger than you were before. The fact that it is happening is proof that it is what you need, not that the universe wants to victimise you.

Choose Your Language Carefully

Monitor your language as you go through your day. Notice in particular how often you might fall into the habit of complaining. It is common for people to label situations, to judge people and to think negatively about what is happening. The problem with doing this is that over time it becomes incorporated into your sense of identity where it plays out endlessly, making you miserable.

Create the intention that from here on, you will cultivate a different way of thinking. When you notice yourself falling into those negative ways of thinking, reject them and notice instead what is inherently good about the situation and focus on that. There is nothing good to be gained from negative self-talk, and everything to be gained from positive self-talk. It is not about feeling self-righteous, rather you focus on the good things that others have done for you.

Commitment to Practice

Form a strong intention to practice gratitude all day every day. Commit to becoming someone who habitually looks on the bright side and finds much to be grateful for.

In my own case, the first thing I do every morning is give thanks for the gift of this day. I sit on the side of the bed and reflect for a few seconds on how fortunate I am to be alive with a functioning body and mind and another day of life in which to use them. It is very good to think of one's purpose in life at this time. Gratitude and a sense of purpose become the informing principle of your day.

Endless Ways

There are endless ways that you can find to cultivate a mind-set of gratitude. It all begins with forming the intention and becoming committed to the idea of making some changes and living your life differently.

Having made the decision, allow yourself the creative freedom to think of ways of doing this. I could tell you things like *just tell people you appreciate them*, or *go for a walk and use the break to do some thinking* and any number of other suggestions. However, you already know what to do deep down. Forming the intention and making the commitment is how you can unlock these ideas. It all begins with *I WILL do this!*

Chapter 4:
Self-Actualization

The process of becoming Self-Actualized inherently cultivates a profound sense of gratitude. It is a by-product of the process. Self-Actualization is becoming the fullest expression of your potential. It is your purpose in life to engage in this process, each of us on our own unique way.

Abraham Maslow is well-known for his work on the hierarchy of human needs. Basic needs must be satisfied before you become aware of higher order needs. The hierarchy is represented as a pyramid, with the basic needs at the pyramid's broad base, and with self-actualisation at the apex.

A Self-Actualised person has found a way to satisfy all of his or her lower needs and has cultivated the conscious awareness of their highest self. They allow this awareness to express itself more fully in their lives.

The achievement of Self-Actualisation is recognised by Maslow as a human need, so in a sense it is everyone's birth right to be self-actualised.

The need for Self-Actualisation asserts itself once we have satisfied the lowest-order needs for food, shelter, sex, then middle-order needs for safety and security, then the higher middle-order needs for love and belonging. Above these is the higher-order need for self-esteem. The highest need of all, sitting like the capstone of a pyramid is the need for Self-Actualisation.

The annals of various religions tell us that a person can achieve the highest expression of their human potential with only some or none of the higher and middle order needs being met, and with only the barest of lower-order needs like food and shelter being satisfied. This is more difficult, requiring you to become an ascetic recluse and engage in mortification of the flesh to free yourself of these normal human needs. The author is *not* recommending this course of action. Our body is not an impediment to self-actualization and happiness. Quite the opposite, it is a great ally. We owe it to ourselves to take the best care of our body that we can by eating well, getting enough exercise and rest, and avoiding toxic and/or addictive substances.

We all have the same set of hierarchical needs but the unique circumstances of our lives means that the way we go about satisfying them will be different for every individual. What follows is not a prescription for achieving self-actualization; rather it is a description of the mind-set of self-actualizing people that anyone can emulate in their own life. It paints a portrait that you can model yourself after.

Experience Things Fully, Vividly, Selflessly

Self-Actualised (SA) people throw themselves wholeheartedly into the experiences that come their way; concentrating on it fully, allowing it to fully absorb them.

The only way this can be done is to be (a) mindful, that is fully conscious in the present moment and (b) fully accepting of the circumstances of that moment. In other words, you are fully aware and accepting of whatever situation you find yourself in.

This is easier said than done because most of the time we impose judgment on situations and in the process we alienate ourselves from it. Soon we are thinking we would like to be somewhere else.

In terms of achieving your full potential, mindfulness is about using an evolved part of your brain that many people do not use. It lays dormant, waiting for the command to awaken.

You can awaken this part of your brain by simply deciding (and following through on the decision) to observe the on-going activity in your own mind. Using a computer metaphor, you activate a monitoring program that watches what is going on.

This phenomenon can be described as metaconsciousness, or thinking about thinking. It is a *new dimension of consciousness* that humans are capable of that no other intelligent species can manage. There is

31

the part of you that thinks your normal thoughts, and then there is the part that observes you thinking those thoughts. Previously there was only the thinker. Now there is the thinker and the observer.

Awakening the observer, this higher dimension of thought, is an important aspect of becoming Self-Actualised.

Mindfulness also helps you to stop thinking so much about the past and the future by removing the dimension of time from your thinking.

In the Now you observe the world of phenomena in a judgment-free way. You accept it without mental resistance, understanding that this resistance is what prevents you from experiencing every moment of your life as the best moment.

On-going Choice Between Safety and Risk

Your life is a moment-by-moment choice between safety (out of fear and need for defence) and risk (for the sake of progress and growth): SA people consciously make the growth choice many times a day.

If you observe your own mind in action (as in previous section) you will notice that this continuum (with safety at one end and risk at the other) is often active in your thinking.

There is a dynamic tension between these two opposites, and you will habitually lean towards one or the other. If you are like many people, you are probably inclined towards the safe, low-risk option because you want predictability and comfort with no unpleasant surprises.

A Self-Actualising person may still value comfort and security, but they know that personal growth is slow for as long as they remain in their comfort-zone. They therefore take themselves out of their comfort zone as often as they can in order to create the right conditions for Self-Actualisation.

A life well-lived will always involve both pleasure and pain. Deep acceptance of this fact is essential for personal growth.

Let Your True Self Emerge

SA people try to go beyond socially-defined modes of thinking and feeling. They let their inner experience tell them what they truly feel.

When in doubt, be honest. It may take some courage, but SA people look honestly at themselves and take responsibility for who they are and what happens to them. Self-delusion is the enemy of self-actualisation.

If you are monitoring your thinking and behaviour, you might notice that much of what you think and do conforms to what you believe people expect of you.

To the greatest extent possible, you should listen to what your intuition is telling you about people and situations and behave according to this more reliable guide. As you become Self-Actualised, the voice of your intuition becomes stronger because you are listening to it more. You recognise it as a reliable, in-built guidance mechanism that always has your best interests foremost.

There are times when we need to conform to certain behavioural standards in order to get along in the world. The challenge is finding a way of harmonising or reconciling what your intuition is telling you and how the world expects you to behave when the two are at variance.

The idea is expressed perfectly in Shakespeare's Hamlet, where Polonius gives this most valuable advice to his son; *This above all: to thine own self be true, And it must follow, as the night the day, Thou canst not then be false to any man.*

Listen To Your Own Tastes

SA people are prepared to be unpopular if necessary.

The SA person does not look for trouble, but when there is a conflict between what they inwardly know is right, and what everyone else is saying, a SA person has the courage to disagree with the group and risk their disapproval or ostracism.

When we receive disapproval, it is profoundly uncomfortable. Most of us will do anything to avoid it. That usually means compliantly going along in order to get along. Disapproval is an instrument of control that opinion-leaders use to enforce conformist behaviour. Membership of a group is contingent on conforming to group norms.

Approval is the other side of the same coin; behaviour that conforms to group expectations is rewarded and reinforced. Approval and disapproval together form the standard "carrot and stick" approach to motivating people.

Group-think and blind conformity is anathema to the SA person.

The SA person recognises when the people around them use approval and/or disapproval to try to influence their behaviour. Their challenge is finding a way to maintain their integrity without creating unnecessary conflict.

Use Your Intelligence

SA people work to do well the things they do, no matter how insignificant those things seem. They understand that greatness comes not so much from what you do, but how well you do the things you do no matter how big or small they are.

SA people know that great satisfaction comes from focussing fully on the task in front of them, and doing that task to the absolute best of their ability.

There is tremendous satisfaction in doing everything as well as you can, even the small, seemingly unimportant things. Doing this keeps your mind firmly in the present moment, the only time and place where you can truly be alive.

The task itself is not as important as the creation in yourself of an attitude of excellence, which is another way of saying living to your fullest potential.

You no longer think that near enough is good enough, that economy of effort and taking it easy as much as you can is the best way to live. These are self-limiting attitudes that will keep you in the realm of mediocrity.

When you live this way, *every moment becomes the best moment of your life.*

Make Peak Experiencing More Likely

Get rid of illusions and false notions. SA people find out what it is they are good at, and what they are not good at.

Being honest with yourself about this is a foundation for Self-Actualisation. SA people are honest, even brutally honest with themselves at every level of their lives. What they aim for is congruency between their inner and outer worlds.

Honesty will eventually create harmony inside and outside of being. Nature cannot lie to itself, but humans do lie to themselves and in so doing create a false inner world. By ridding yourself of delusion, your inner world comes into alignment with the outer world, creating harmony.

So, honesty creates the right conditions to have deep insight into the nature of the world you live in. This is the insight that leads you to Self-Actualisation.

Know Thyself

SA people ask themselves who are you, what are you, what is good and what is bad for you, where you are going, what is your mission?

Opening yourself up like this allows you to recognize your defences that stand in the way of ultimate fulfilment. The challenge then is to find the courage to let them go.

Coming to deep self-knowledge is a life-time endeavour. In ancient times, it was believed that only by knowing your inner world, the microcosm, can you come to have knowledge of the outer world, the macrocosm. The micro is a miniature of the macro, correct in every detail in the way that a fragment of a hologram contains full detail of the whole.

Characteristics of Self-Actualised People

This section outlines the characteristics shared by self-actualizing people everywhere, regardless of culture.

Realistically oriented with an efficient perception of reality extending into all areas of life. SA people are unthreatened by the unknown. They have a superior ability to think clearly and logically, allowing them to arrive at an understanding of the truth of a situation.

Accept oneself, others and the natural world the way they are. SA people see human nature as it really is, not as the people around them think it ought to be. Furthermore they have rid themselves of crippling guilt; they act with integrity in the way they know is right and are therefore able to enjoy themselves without regret or apology. They have no unnecessary inhibitions.

Spontaneous in their inner life, thoughts and impulses. SA people are unhampered by convention. Their ethics are autonomous, they see themselves as an individual, and are motivated towards continual improvement.

Focus on problems outside oneself. SA people have a mission in life that requires much energy; their mission is their reason to live. Sure of its rightness, they are usually serene and worry-free as they pursue their mission with unstoppable determination.

Detachment, the need for privacy. Alone but not lonely, SA people retain their composure amid confusion and personal misfortunes. They are like the hero of Rudyard Kipling's poem If ... *if you can keep your head when all about you are losing theirs and blaming it on you.* SA people are self-starters, responsible for themselves. They own their behaviour.

Autonomous, independent of culture and environment. SA people rely on their inner self for satisfaction. Resilient and stable in the face of hard knocks, SA people are self-contained, independent from the love and respect of others in the sense that they can resist attempts to use these to manipulate them.

Freshness of appreciation. SA people have a fresh rather than stereotyped appreciation of people and things. Moment to moment living is thrilling, transcendent and spiritual. SA people live the present moment to the fullest.

Peak experiences. In Maslow's words *"Feelings of limitless horizons opening up to the vision, the feeling of being simultaneously more powerful and also more helpless than one ever was before, the feeling of ecstasy and wonder and awe, the loss of placement in time and space with, finally, the conviction that something extremely important and valuable had happened, so that the subject was to some extent transformed and strengthened even in his daily life by* *such experiences. When peak experiences are especially powerful, the sense of self dissolves into an awareness of a greater unity."* (from Religion, Values and Peak Experiences, 1970).

The way Maslow describes Self-Actualised people is very similar to the way a person who has achieved Satori in Zen is described. They are qualitatively the same experience. This is a natural human state, albeit a one that few people have yet reached, but one which is achievable with commitment and effort.

Chapter 5:
Lifestyle

Maintaining an on-going feeling of gratitude for your life will be greatly improved by being as healthy as you can be. To the fullest extent possible, you should try to adopt a healthy life-style. This chapter outlines the ways that people everywhere have used to optimise their health.

Have an Annual Health Check

Your health is *your* responsibility, not your doctor's or anyone else. Take control by scheduling an annual wellness check-up with your doctor to actively work towards maintaining good health. Do not wait until you get sick to visit the doctor.

In my own case, I go to see my doctor every year in January for my annual well-ness check. She performs a full range of checks for a man my age and gives advice -- which I make sure I follow. Doing this means I stay healthy and do not need any further visits. This is proactive health management versus reactive management.

Proactively avoid becoming sick by having the doctor give you a thorough check-up to identify potential problems before they become an *actual* problem. For example, your blood pressure or cholesterol may be too high, you may be heading towards diabetes, your prostate might be enlarged, there might be polyps growing in your large intestine, there may be a lump in your breast. All of these are treatable, but can be fatal if left too long.

If your parents or grandparents are deceased, what was the cause of death? What about uncles and aunts, great-uncles and aunts on both sides of the family. As the old saying goes, *the apple does not fall far from the tree*. This will give you a good indication of what your most likely problems are going to be.

Walk at Least 30 Minutes a Day

Walking is the perfect exercise. Our bodies have evolved to walk long distances; though a sedentary lifestyle may make the idea of walking several kilometres a day seem much too strenuous.

Walking is classed as aerobic exercise. This improves the efficiency of your lungs to absorb oxygen, and your heart's ability to pump that oxygen to all parts of your body. Walking does not just exercise your legs. Your upper body is also participating; you swing your arms and rotate your trunk as you go.

Walking is also an opportunity to notice the myriad things, large and small, that exist unnoticed in your environment. It is worth it because there is extraordinary beauty just waiting to be experienced.

Don't just walk with tunnel vision; look about you, hear the sounds, smell the smells, notice the complex patterns of Nature. Look for the beauty that is all around. As the old saying goes, *what you seek is also seeking you*. Do you want beautiful things to manifest in your life? Seek them out, and they will find you.

Take your time, be in the moment, cultivate a sense of gratitude that you are alive and able to walk around. You will be richly rewarded if you do this.

This kind of mindful walking can be the foundation of your daily exercise regime. Around 30 minutes a day or more gives you the required amount of aerobic exercise while nourishing your mind and spirit.

Sense of Humour

Laughter is a universal human phenomenon. Everyone, everywhere instinctively does it, and understands why others do it, regardless of language or culture. Science does not have a good understanding of why we laugh, but it has been recognised that it is a key element in social bonding. We like people who make us laugh. Incidentally, it is thought that the origins of laughter are in releasing the tension and expressing the shared relief at the passing of danger.

The ability to see the humorous side of life is about resiliency. Humour has a curiously life-enhancing effect because it requires an optimistic mind-set.

Laughter is a natural way for you to experience free and simple enjoyment of life. Research shows that it directly creates a range of healthy physical changes in the body. It strengthens the immune system, releases endorphins that promotes feelings of well-being and reduces pain, improves blood circulation, boosts energy, reduces conflict between people and overall works to lessen the damaging effects of stress.

A good belly-laugh relaxes your whole body, making it an effective remedy for stress. It has a strengthening effect on the immune system by decreasing the stress hormones that may be present. When these stress hormones are present, the immune system has a more difficult task in fighting infection.

Laughter releases endorphins -- these are naturally released under a variety of circumstances including exercise, excitement (for example laughter), pain, consumption of spicy food, love and sexual excitement. Endorphins produce an analgesic effect and a feeling of well-being.

Laughter protects the heart. Laughter improves the function of blood vessels and increases blood flow, which can help protect you against a heart attack and other cardiovascular problems. Try to adopt a mind-set that can appreciate the funny side of life.

Maintain an Active Lifestyle

The best kind of exercise is natural movement that is an integral part of your normal lifestyle. Going to the gymnasium, performing a daily exercise regime might be enjoyable for highly disciplined people, but the majority of us will struggle to maintain any exercise regime over years and decades. It seems too much like hard work.

Exercise regimes are unnecessary if your life involves a moderate amount of natural, low-impact movement such as walking, swimming, cycling, gardening or anything else you like. The key is to *enjoy* it. You will want to keep doing what you enjoy.

Avoid high-impact sports that stress bones and joints. Over time, those joints will wear out and become inflamed and painful due to overuse. Remember, people in the evolutionary past rarely lived past middle age, so while they often had to exert themselves greatly, their bodies did not need to last very long by today's standards.

You cannot keep doing the strenuous things you used to do when you were young and expect your body to keep working. Expending upwards of 3,000 to 3,500 calories over the course of the day will give you the right balance.

Studies have shown that inactive people do not live as long as active people, and the group that lives the longest burns about 3,000 to 3,500 calories per day.

Be a Gardener

Related to the previous section, gardening is one of the best possible ways of getting the physical exercise you need while doing something enjoyable.

There is something profoundly satisfying about cultivating plants in your own garden. Beyond the obvious benefits of creating your own super-fresh food, it is profoundly satisfying at an instinctive level to dig in the earth, feel the texture of it in your hands, smell those earthy smells, plant seeds, water them, watch them grow, pull out weeds and so on. Being an unhurried gardener can add years to your life.

Exercise Your Brain

No less important than exercising your body is exercising your brain. Your brain consumes around 30% of your body's energy, far greater than any other organ.

Nearly a third of all of the energy created by the digestion of food goes to generating the electrical impulses of the brain and central nervous system. Simply put, your brain is an expensive organ to run, so it is not surprising that people have a tendency to use it less. But to stay young and live long, it is vitally important that the brain be kept fully functional and not allowed to wither away through not enough use.

46

Find something new and interesting to occupy your mind with every day. It does not matter too much what it is, though it helps if you consider it to be meaningful and contributing to your purpose in life.

Keep learning; learn a new language, a musical instrument, take up a hobby, do crosswords and jig-saw puzzles. Do any or all of these things and more to keep your brain young.

Build Strong Bones

Strong bones can be built through daily activity that exerts weight on the bones. As with every other part of your body, if you do not use it, you lose it. Astronauts who spend extended periods of weightlessness are known to suffer from a marked decrease in bone density because their bodies no longer need the bone density needed on Earth.

Sitting in an armchair or lying on a couch all day is telling your body that it does not need strong bones, so your bone density adjusts to what it needs to be for a sedentary lifestyle.

Keep Your Expectations Low

It has been wisely said that the secret of a long and happy life is to keep your expectations low. You are rarely disappointed and so will avoid getting angry.

Often, you will be pleasantly surprised when your low expectations are exceeded.

Look around you in the world. The people who complain the most, who express their unhappiness with life are those whose expectations have not been met. Perhaps they were too high in the first place, or perhaps they really did get a raw deal. Either way, being angry and inflicting negativity helps no-one. If there really has been an injustice, it can be settled amicably. There is no need to become a door-mat when maintaining low expectations.

Get Some Sun, But Not Too Much

The sun is the source of almost all life on Earth. We definitely need it in our life if we are not to suffer from Vitamin D deficiency which leads to Rickets.

Depending on how much melanin pigmentation you have in your skin, for good health you need to get some exposure to the sun, preferably every day. Too much sun is a leading cause of skin cancer. In the Australian state of Queensland (where I live) the sun is strong and many people have Scottish ancestry with its red hair and pale skin that freckles not tans when exposed to strong sun. Consequently, Queensland has one of the highest rates of skin cancer anywhere in the world, much higher than in Scotland. For people with fair skin, no more than a few minutes a day of direct exposure to the sun without protection are likely to cause problems in the long-term. People with brown or dark brown skin can tolerate more sun.

Massage

Therapeutic massage is both relaxing and healing. There is something fundamental in human nature that responds positively to touch. Children who receive too little nurturing touch may survive physically, but their emotional development will have been seriously impaired.

Unfortunately the term 'massage' has become synonymous with various forms of sexual activity. While I acknowledge the beneficial effects of sexual release for those who need it, the kind of massage being discussed here is of the Swedish, Thai, shiatsu, acupressure kind. These work on a whole of body level to improve the circulation of blood and lymph, release of muscular tension and promote a general sense of well-being.

Listen to Calming Music

Soothing, gentle music is therapeutic because it lessens tension. At a cognitive level, it helps with memory, concentration and reasoning skills. At a physical level, it lowers your blood pressure, elevates your mood, relaxes your muscles and boosts your immune system.

All in all, there is no down-side to listening to calming music. The same cannot be said for highly stimulating music that is fast and frantic. Music is essentially an emotional statement. Your inner world will resonate to the mood of the music being listened to.

Be Flexible in Your Thinking

Related to the previous point, being flexible, like a child is flexible, is an essential aspect of healthy aging. When life serves up a situation that is not what you expect or are accustomed to, do not become cranky and negative. If you cannot change the situation, have the grace to simply accept it with good humour.

Rid Yourself of Addiction

Easier said than done, yet smoking, excessive alcohol consumption or over-consumption of a wide-range of illicit and prescription drugs has a strongly adverse effect on your mental and physical health.

For more detailed information see David Tuffley's book *Beating Addiction*.

Ease into the Day

Upon waking in the morning, try not to launch too quickly or energetically into the day. The strain of going from a dormant state to heightened activity can heavily tax your organs, particularly the heart.

The majority of heart attacks and strokes occur in the morning. Go to bed early enough so that you can get up early enough the next morning to give yourself time to ease into the day, rather than sleep in as late as possible, then have to frantically launch into your morning's activities.

The Flame that Burns Twice as Bright

The flame that burns twice as bright burns half as long, as the saying goes. Try to pace yourself to a steady, even pace and avoid extremes if you possibly can. This includes matching your diet with your lifestyle.

If you are relatively inactive, eat a light, preferably vegetarian diet. If you are physically active, a higher protein diet is needed. Eating a high protein, high calorie diet with a sedentary lifestyle will cause weight-gain.

Snoring and Sleep Apnoea

Sleep apnoea is condition where a person stops breathing for a short period while asleep, following by a loud snort as the person gasps for breath. This event can be repeated between 5 and 30 times per hour.

Snoring and sleep apnoea obviously disrupt your breathing while you are unconscious. To starve your body of oxygen while sleeping is obviously not a good thing. It raises your blood pressure and also raises the level of cholesterol in the blood too, leading to a heightened risk of heart attack and stroke. People who die in their sleep often do so as a result of these. Seek medical advice if you suffer from either of these.

Take a Siesta

Studies show that a short nap of about 45 minutes or less (one sleep cycle) in the middle of the day has a highly beneficial effect on a person's health.

Latin cultures have no difficulty accepting the wisdom of this practice. Anglo cultures on the other hand tend to regard a midday snooze as a sign of laziness; hence Noel Coward's whimsical song *mad dogs and Englishmen go out in the midday sun.*

Lose weight and do your heart a favour

It is not difficult to see how carrying around an additional 20 or 30 kilograms can place great strain on your heart. Imagine permanently carrying a back-pack weighing that much. It would be ridiculous and intolerable to place such a handicap on you, yet this is exactly what many people are doing in our obesity-afflicted Western world.

In the course of evolution, humans developed the ability to store body fat because famine was a very real danger. Today, in the absence of some catastrophic event that disrupts society, we are always going to be able to find enough to eat.

Losing weight is easier said than done. Our eating habits become very deeply embedded and are highly resistant to change. Your doctor can advise the best course of action for your situation.

Pace Yourself

When you have a job that requires much physical and/or mental effort, do not try to do it all in one session. You might wish to get it done and out of the way, but the excessive effort will put your body under stress.

Adjust your expectations about how soon the job needs to be finished. Allow it to be open-ended. Then approach the job in manageable chunks. Work for an hour, then rest, work another hour, rest again. Pacing yourself in this way is being kind to your body and avoids over-straining.

Avoid Eating to Ease Emotional Pain

It is well-known that comfort foods like chocolate and other high fat, high sugar and high salt foods can give temporary relief for emotional upset, but at what cost to your health?

Often the habit is established and reinforced in childhood when you were given treats to cheer you up when you were upset, often by somebody that you trusted uncritically.

When done to excess, this is a form of binge eating and really should be brought under control as it will lead to obesity and diabetes. If you address the underlying issue, the food addiction will become manageable. See Appendix C for advice on overcoming addiction.

Aromatherapy

Our sense of smell is tied to a very primitive part of our brain, the so-called 'lizard brain'. The lizard brain operates mostly below the level of conscious thought. It makes its presence felt as powerful emotion.

Smells can therefore exert a powerful influence on our mood. Use this knowledge to your advantage by arranging your living space to have aromas that make you feel calm and relaxed.

There are many helpful books on aromatherapy that you can easily access. In summary though, jasmine helps with depression, lavender with sleeplessness, citrus for mental alertness, peppermint and ginger for poor digestion, eucalyptus for sinus problems. Avoid pungent, unpleasant smells if possible.

Remain Sexually Active

Healthy sexual activity has been compared to the fountain of youth. Sexual intimacy makes us feel connected with and loved by another person. Sex releases a potent cocktail of natural, feel-good substances into the bloodstream (endorphins, DHEA and growth hormone) that promote health and a sense of well-being. These counteract the stress hormones adrenalin and cortisol which may be present as a result of life's trials and tribulations.

There are three basic guidelines that will ensure a positive experience; both parties must be willing participants, be intuitive and spontaneous about what you do and how you do it, and make sure you are meeting your partner's needs as well as your own.

Nurture Loving Family Relationships

Being on close, loving terms with your family has been shown by studies to lengthen a person's life and to improve the quality of that life by creating a strong sense of community, belonging and mutual support.

Be a Good Neighbour

Neighbours are members of your extended family in the sense that what affects you, also affects them. Try to build a relationship of mutual respect and support if necessary. Good neighbours can greatly add to your quality of life. Ask yourself, 'if I had myself as a neighbour, what would I think of me?' Try to be the neighbour that you yourself would want.

Do Not Hold Grudges

Staying angry and holding grudges against people who have done you harm will only succeed in making you sick in the medium to long term. As the old saying goes, being angry with someone is like drinking poison and expecting the other person to die. As difficult as it might be, you MUST let your grievances go if you are to live a long and happy life. Forgiving does not mean forgetting and allowing the same problem to happen again. You need never allow that problem to happen again. it is essential though that you let the past go. Concentrate on what is happening in the present moment and think as little as possible about the past.

Try to Understand, not Judge

As Stephen Covey pointed out, when a person is busy judging others, they are unable to empathise and understand the others. Judgment and understanding are mutually exclusive mind-sets. Making a judgment is to say 'I know everything I need to know about this situation. My mind is now closed to new information.'

Use empathy often to cultivate understanding and compassion for others in the world. They are not so very different from you. If you were in their situation, you might very well act the same.

Self-Reliance

Long-lived people tend to be fiercely independent. They do not expect others to do for them what they are able to do for themselves. The activity and energy required to take care of their daily chores helps to keep them fit.

One reason long-lived people can still take care of themselves in advanced old age is because they have simplified their lives to the point where there is not overly much to do, just a few simple rituals such as tending the garden, going for a walk, feeding the chickens. Cultivate a simple, modest life without a lot of clutter or reliance on consumer goods.

Chapter 6:
Mindfulness Meditation Practice

Many readers will already be practicing meditation, and need no further encouragement to do this most beneficial of activities. If you already have a meditation regime, or would like to improve on what you are already doing, or if you do not meditate at all, this chapter outlines the distilled essence of mindfulness meditation practice.

Once you know the essential basics, you can adapt the technique to suit your needs. Meditation is something that can be learned in a few minutes, but which can take a lifetime to perfect. *The greater the truth, the more simply it can be expressed*. Think of Einstein's $E=mc^2$ equation (the energy contained in an object equals the mass of the object multiplied by the square of the speed of light). This is a great, fundamental truth that has been expressed very simply which gives it great impact. Einstein could have said it in 100,000 words and the statement would be just as true, but the impact would be far less because so many people would not have penetrated to the heart of this truth.

Meditation establishes primary attention on your inner self where it should be. It allows you to shift your attention away from the clamouring demands of a complex outer world with its strident messages and competing demands. When you meditate every day, you can continue to live in the material world, but that world is placed into its proper perspective as your secondary reality.

Meditation creates a peaceful inner space within which you can become aware of the more subtle aspects of yourself that have been hitherto obscured by the noise of the outer world. In this space, your intuition grows stronger, revealing to you a rich stream of subtle but powerful knowledge to help you germinate the seeds of enlightenment that lie ready in you. Meditation is free and completely natural.

Simple method for meditation

Meditation is heightened awareness without the mental chatter.

With our restless minds in control and demanding entertainment, it may seem that meditation is difficult. Plus there are so many approaches a person can take. It is good to know that there is a very simple and effective method that anyone can use, almost anytime they want. It is the essence of every meditation method, and is so simple that it only takes a few minutes to learn, though perhaps a lot longer to master.

Begin by sitting comfortably and begin to breathe rhythmically. Sit with spine straight but in a way that will not induce sleep. Breathe deeply, from the diaphragm, in through your nose and out through your mouth. Breathing is really the key here. The fresh oxygen that enters your bloodstream has an almost immediate, beneficial effect, inducing a sense of well-being. But be careful of your posture. If you are too comfortable sleep will not be far away. Sleep is definitely not meditation. Sleep is unconsciousness, not heightened consciousness.

Focus your conscious awareness on the place immediately behind the centre of your forehead, the so-called third eye. This is the place that mystics believe is the seat of the soul, or highest self. Imagine that in this place there is a crystal about the size of a marble. There is a whole universe contained in that crystal, a perfect, scaled-down copy of the larger universe. Feel the crystal warming up, beginning to glow. The glow becomes a powerful beacon of light, radiating out in all directions, getting brighter and stronger, bathing your body and everything around you with pure loving energy. Your highest self is doing this. You have a powerful desire to bring your highest self into your everyday awareness.

After centering your awareness and then allowing it to expand outwards, continue to consciously **breathe deeply and rhythmically**. Concentrate your awareness on the in-breath without engaging in any mental commentary. Simply be aware of the breath as it comes in, and be likewise aware as it goes out, all the while remaining centred, aware and thoughtless. This rhythmic breathing and focussed awareness is the essence of meditation. Practicing this alone will give you as much benefit as the many courses offered by new age organisations.

You can **count sub-vocally on the out-breath** up to a certain number of breaths, (say 50). Or you can set a timer to remind you when ten minutes has passed. Ten minutes is a good duration to begin with. Do the ten minutes for two weeks or so until it becomes well-established, then gradually increase the duration up to 30 minutes over the weeks that follow.

Your goal should be to **meditate in this way for up to 30 minutes, twice a day.** It is good to begin your day with a meditation session. Likewise end the day with a session in the evening not long before bed-time.

Of course, as you get used to your meditation practice, and start to feel the benefits (stress reduction, more even-tempered, expanded awareness, intuitive insights, increased creativity, improved relationships, enjoyment of life, to name a few) you may feel inclined to take some time during the day to meditate, say at lunch time. Just choose a safe place where you won't be disturbed for half an hour, if that is possible. Even if it is not, you can snatch a few minutes here and there and still derive worthwhile benefit.

How do you know if you are doing it right? Remember, meditation is heightened awareness without the mental chatter. If you can get yourself into a state of heightened awareness and are able to quiet your mind of the chatter for a period of time, then you are meditating. By doing this, you switch off the ego, activate the part of the brain where higher awareness is lives, and flush your body with plenty of oxygen. It is enough to make you feel relaxed with a deep sense of well-being.

Meditating for a short time is not difficult. Doing it for 15 or 20 minutes twice a day for the rest of your life will be more challenging. Resolve to meditate regularly for two weeks. Fourteen days, that is not too much to commit to. At the end of this time, you should be feeling the benefits for yourself at a deep level, and this might be enough to establish meditation as a permanent part of your life.

Practice non-attachment

One of the hardest things about meditation is an undisciplined mind that insists on being listened to and entertained. A mind that generates random thoughts about all manner of things, a mind which jumps from one thought to another like a grasshopper. This describes most people, most of the time.

No matter how interesting or important or disturbing these thoughts might be, when meditating it is important that you do not allow your attention to latch onto these random thoughts. Imagine that they are like loose pages of a newspaper blowing in the wind. Allow the wind to carry the newspaper away and give them no further thought. Resist the impulse to catch the page and read the worldly news written upon it. Understand that all such news is short-lived and ultimately without any real substance. In other words, practice what Zen Masters would call non-attachment. Attachment to worldly things is a major cause of human suffering, since nothing in the world is permanent. That which we are attached to must soon change or disappear, and we suffer because what we were attached to is now gone. Practicing non-attachment removes the cause of suffering. Another way to look at this is to practice having very low expectations. With low expectations you will seldom if ever be disappointed. Non-attachment is the key to meditation. It is also the key to a contented, if not happy life in general.

Conclusion

This book presents information and strategies to help you deal with the challenging events that come your way in life. Losing your job or business, relationship break-up, bereavement, illness or disability, and being the victim of crime are all examples of situations where when resilience should come to the fore.

How would *you* react to events of this seriousness? Would it knock the wind out of you such that you would find it difficult to carry on? Or do you have the resilience to get up again and keep moving forwards?

This book aims to help you be the kind of person who bounces back and carries on, stronger than before. It describes what resilience is and how you can cultivate it in your own life so that you can meet those catastrophic events and go on to become a stronger, happier person.

I wish you the very best on your journey.

The End

About the Author

David Tuffley PhD is a Lecturer in Applied Ethics & Socio-Technical Studies at Griffith University in Australia. David has written widely on Applied Psychology topics.

For other books written in the Applied Psychology and other series, visit David's Amazon Author site. (Google on *david tuffley amazon author*)

Join him on Facebook at **facebook.com/tuffley**

www.ingramcontent.com/pod-product-compliance
Lightning Source LLC
Chambersburg PA
CBHW071236280526
45787CB00002B/957